INSIDE
DARK
LIGHT

INSIDE DARK LIGHT
Lucky Ryder

Also by Lucky:

These Things I Crave
Water Media
Violent Words for Beautiful People
O.G. Indigo

Contact: sakulryder@gmail.com

Portrait taken by
Sienna St. Laurent

Inside Dark Light
©2021 Lucky Ryder

ISBN 978-1-7774688-0-4

All rights reserved.

No part of this publication may be reproduced, distributed or transmitted in any form or by any means, electronic, mechanical, photocopying, recording or otherwise, without the prior written permission of the author.

CONTENTS

11	OPENINGS
12	THE GAP YOU LEAVE BEHIND
14	DRAGGING BELLS
16	DIALATION MATERIAL
17	HOLY TOMB
18	PENDULUM
21	LOOK WHAT HAPPENS WHEN THE SUN COMES OUT
23	THE DIVIDING POOL
24	AIR ON AIR
26	NEW GROUNDS
27	POST
29	BIG TOP
30	WHOLE
31	WRITING IN SILENCE
32	ONE TUSK ONE TONGUE
38	THE ROOT AND THE ROOF
41	EMPTINESS IS FORM
44	BEARS
46	CANYONS
47	FIRST, TIE THE LACES
50	OF STONE AND SILK

51	ONE LAST TOON
53	BOOKS ON BENCHES
54	TROUBLE MAKERS
56	PENTAGRAM
57	ELBOW LAKE
58	ZOMBIE
59	BLOSSOM
60	WITH BATED BREATH
61	TREMULANT
62	WAX
63	ROSE
65	CATACOMBS
66	WORN
69	THE FIELD THE WHEAT THE SICKLE THE SWING THE DULLING THE CASH THE INJURY REPEAT
72	COLOR OF THE STAIN
73	APERTURE
75	OYEZ
77	INTENTION
78	FOSTER
80	MURDER ISLAND
81	SWORDFISH
82	LITTLE BOAT

Your beauty requires
no acknowledgement.

Your art, no audience.

If no one ever visits.
If no one ever sees.
If no one ever comes.

The lotus still grows.

OPENINGS

To live in the static
and be in the rap,
when the web fell apart
and the beat, it collapsed.

Something funny
happened when I said
fuck it, I'm done;

the melody bloomed,
and I found I'd begun...

THE GAP YOU LEAVE BEHIND

You leave a gap
only the archer's towers
have ever come to know.

The singing arc
of the sound
of a single arrow
separating the skin,
only slightly.

The silence that remains
thrashes loudly in the net
of attention that had been caught,
and the stone and dirt underfoot
billow softly like wood that
knows the fire to come.

The distance cracks,
leaving iron slaked upon
your still wrought tongue.
The taste so familiar,
the kin of coal and mud
and warm pale palms pressed
against your lips no more.

On this side of the mountains,
the last glimpsing hues of day
are withheld and bid gaze upon
the gloaming clasped around
your shoulders, and reaching out to
where sight no longer dares to tread.

This planet is a sphere.
The sun will rise again.
Your eyes will squint and dilate,
and the gap you leave
will wear a different skin.

DRAGGING BELLS

Dragging bells out from
under where the sky hung.

Their tones are a woven cloak
pulled out by the eyelids.

Echoing against the cliffs
a silver tongue floods from
the slash in a fawn's throat.

Ground into soot and dust.
Cracked stone, and from
the surrounding trunks
the earth heaves.
She erupts with bones
and the bones breathe.

A wide swath swoons through the
woods and an old stream rises again.
A song only silence has ever been
one to stir; emerges, unfurls,
and in the shade, remains.

One day it will break the skin.
The seam between will be eaten away,

and all that frays will reach
out to touch everything
and we will exhale only glass.

As the thick, black,
clean soil absorbs us,
a new constellation
is quietly born deep
in the edgeless layers.

Steeped by the burgeoning
warrens heady with skulls
diffusing all the nerve ends,
and sloughing off the corpses
at only the points of contact.

Dust and fog lift from the forest
as the earth shudders and
the young starry-eyed ghosts
take residence
in the fresh openings,
quickly,
before she settles.

DILATION MATERIAL

There are ways to free our minds from the
arrest of stimulus without losing presence.

We can augment our experience through decisive input,
and by giving witness to how the impact of the lens
under which we perceive our relationships, alters
the manner in which we seek out source material.

There is bedrock that these sources project from,
and at the times when the veil thins
and we are able to press ourselves against it,
we find that our beings adhere,
all the same.

What we garner is dependent on dilation of the aperture
and subjective receptivity of the sensory organism.
No matter how deeply we coalesce,
the potential for variable, dwindles not.

To free our minds, we must surrender
to the space that exists therein.

The entity that forms between us,
our surrender, and that space.
There are those who call it god.

HOLY TOMB

Holy tomb
dark at noon,
give us pause
in the light of day.
Bid us one with
breath and pulse
until all life
is stripped away.

PENDULUM

I,
am the way things were.
To long for me is to dishonor
the holiness of all that is fleeting.

To mediate guilt into your longing
is to disrespect the staccato pendulum
of your cracking soul.

So shatter on my brothers and sisters.

Blow away like stardust
and return as a comet
breaking up upon re-entry.
Scatter through the cosmos with
your eyes shut and your lips parted.

Spread your wings beyond your being.
Let the pieces lay where they fall.
Keep your kiss sacred and
gift your blood unto the masses.

Scream like honey and whisper barbed wire secrets
into the whiskey of your friends. So that in their dreams,
the shadows of nightmares will smell you on their breath

and know that those you drink with
are not to be fucked with. And if they still do,
goddamn they'll fucking know that we are not alone.

Sing along to deep bass music that has no words.

Press your body against the speaker
and imagine how our elder's bones
tremor inside the ground
every time the earth quakes.

Find sanctuary in the fact that you,
are all that you will ever really have,
and quite frankly,
you probably never had that either.

So betray yourself.
Burn your writing, bury your art
and throw your altar into the ocean.
Dance on your own grave. Curse your home
and bask in the precious moment
after saying the wrong thing.

Raise your fists to the sky like the weapons
they are and lay your breath amongst the reeds
of another night's rain and another dawn's fog.

Never look away and never look back.

Pray that they will all blame you, because at the end of it,
you know you have the strength to swaddle yourself
in a thousand shades of forgiveness and cradle your
misplaced and precarious mange, late into the gloaming.

Tear the hardware from the straight jacket.
Dig your kicks into the concrete, and let your lungs
go nuclear against the rattling of an army of hope
carved from splintered ivory collapsing outwards.

Let entropy be the perpetually focused bloom
of a victorious hill top on which you stand.
For there are wars to be fought,
and defeat is not optional.

Let the demons know there is
a feast waiting at the end of you,
and thank the angels
for their work in its preparation.

LOOK WHAT HAPPENS WHEN THE SUN COMES OUT

Look what happens when the sun comes out.
We turn our bellies to the shiny rays.
We gape and yawn and fill our mouths.
Our little furry hands we splay.
Stretching up towards the sky,
the dewy beads evaporate.

The warmth soaks in, the cold
of the previous night is shaken off,
is slaked away. The ground awakes.
The visibility of our breath evades.
Through the obfuscating angles
though as natural in the dark it be,
we permeate this concrete jungle
and its halogenic canopy.

What could we be?

Through the fog and steam
and sharp wide seams between the trees,
we seem to see so much differently.

Take the kaleidoscoping forest filter
as a part of our tetrachromacy,

for everything that's to be seen, we see.

Sub-ceiling. Sub-base. Sub-terra. Sub-nature.

We rub our grippy little fingertips along the bark.

The core experiences touch
like the skin can sense the heart.

Synapses flash like
the fur's own fire sparks.

Mycelium communicates in time
with the pinching birth of stars.

Sub. Base. Core. Word. Crown.

We gather up the simple elements
that draw us near to propagate.

A single dimension
we could not possibly
alone through walk.
Proliferate.

THE DIVIDING POOL

Your ghost
is not
a reflection
of you
that gets
left behind.

Your ghost
is a projection
of a part
of others,
that walks
beside them
now that
you're gone.

AIR ON AIR

I'm still hearing voices, but I'm making better choices.

I'm making the broken windows into art instead of dragging them across my skin. I'm getting closer to the source. Learning not to fear the truth in me. Teaching myself to be a healer, but sometimes given ritual, I'm not afraid to bleed.

I'm incinerating my past. I pour the ashes on the glass, with my feather quill I split the pile down the middle, right in half. In glass vials I keep a portion, dangling around my painted neck. The rest I throw across the room, I torch the house and all that mess.

There's gasoline in my footprints,
and concentric circles in the skies.
The blade I drop it does not shimmer.
It withers and my knuckles writhe.

And I'm still hearing voices,
but this time I'm talking back.

I separate the tools from the poisons and the nooses from the whips and racks. I wipe the dust from the bottles and find some time and space to drink alone.

I let the candles burn until the wax builds me a throne.
And there are geodes inside my fucking lungs,
the crystals crack every time I die. Every time I wake,
I'm reborn and have to relearn how to fly. I've taken
off so many times, I no longer fear the distance
between the earth and the sky.

I'm falling down.
I'm falling up.
I'm falling right beside my love.
I'm spinning like a weapon catastrophic from above.
Spinning through the atmosphere, the highest peaks
and molten plains. Ripping through the prairie air
and the sound of music that remains.

And no I don't give a damn
about where or how I land,
because when the dust finally settles,
you'll see the man I am.

I'm a burning bush. A falcon's rush. A steel spiderweb
with those little broken bottle panes. I'm a sin with
weight, a dark wood crate, beetles pouring out the
mezzanine. I'm both those bibles. Heaven's hell hole.
The .45's flashing halo. A katana's curve.
A monk that learns; sometimes,
you just have to get a little blood upon the spurs.

NEW GROUNDS

Where a fear to
tread once trembled;

everything I do now,
is a sigh of relief.

POST

There's a wolf at the mouth of the mountain,
and a hunger inside that has resided for so long
that it no longer drives, it has rooted.

It is strings.

It is music in the throat that can't find the tongue,
and the reflection of the blade as it rides alongside the
swerving of the clutch and the seething of the windpipe.

Asphalt and taillights.

A blur and then silence.

Breath in the cold.

Claw marks, candlelit and sacred on the side of the
broken neck of the highway, where the pinching point
met the firing pin and the engine hung in space.

The exhaust beneath the starlight, frozen in place.

The elders drew it out in song
until the skin was left to waste.
In the wake of the shadows and the fires

the contrast took them both,
and left language in their place,
thunder where the quills lived
and no hands beyond the wrists.

A predator on the horizon
who doesn't have to move.
I am coming for that beast.
I am blind and written soon.

There is no hurry, no time stamp
accompanying the photograph.
Just a muddled scroll in the corner
where the walls have never met.
Fingertips on pots and pans and
the absent sun of summer cut from
the starving stomach where it set.

Exhausted, and appropriate,
the quiet find their dawn in
the journey amongst the steep slopes.
Where every sharp turn reveals
a wolf at the mouth of the mountain,
and a hunger inside
that has resounded so deeply,
that it no longer drives,
it has rooted.

BIG TOP

Clay in the rain.
Grain in the stone.
Home in the ash.
Crash in the dome.
Throne in the grave.
Rave in the pit.
Spit in the palm.
Psalm in the fist.

Laughing at sculptures
that came from the cliffs.

Wingspan like vultures
erupting in fits.

Pack up my corpus
and peck at the grits.

Our greatest opus
will remain unspoken,
yet scattered like tokens.

What a circus this is.

WHOLE

That night the lasers spoke for you.

Dulled by the familiar scratching of raised claws
silhouetted by aerosol flame throwers lethargically
burning the twilight oil.

Anxiously picking at the seams between weekends.
Pausing only to raise another dreary cereal filled jaw
to let out the occasional convivial yawn.

Those lasers can go fuck themselves.

Your self stretches out to a point
where its intricate simplicity
will out do the pretty lights
in the forest, on the strip
and in the sky,
every damn time.

So lay down the gusto and come to me.

The holodeck is most beautiful
when no programs are run.

WRITING IN SILENCE

I want to learn to write and speak
in the language of the silence
that came before me.
I want to learn of the space
that I will leave when I am gone.

I want to learn
of the silence
that came before me.
I want to learn of the space
that I will leave.

I want to learn of silence.
I want to learn of space.

Learn of silence.
Of space.

Silence.

Space.

Sil   .

.

ONE TUSK ONE TONGUE

I broke through the floorboards beneath
my bed and I ate the fucking shadows.
I transplanted planks for my forearms
and diary hinges for my elbows.
Now I'm scrawling mystic channel speech
an inch deep into the drywall.
The pure white light is creeping through
and I'm fearing for my dark soul.
Fearing for the jaws and dry bones
I got locked inside of bottles
in the basement of my hostel.
Sure, the place is vacant but I got
too much invested in my vagrancy,
and I'm straight up scared of change
and the possibility of healing.

It feels like the shrapnel
has completely over grown me.

I'd bounce out the back
but it's as bright as the front
with a shine slipping
across the ceiling.
On one knee I'm melting
and burning at the seams.

Screaming, this shed will be my grave.
Little did I know how easily
the coffin inward staved.

I'm carving off the angles
and I'm rounding out my house.
I'm putting out the fires
in the eyes of all my ghosts.
All the metal, all the wolves,
likened to what's biting me.
The dark's been costing
but little did I know,
the fight of the light
from the lightning is free.

It's time, let's eat.
Prying picket fences
from the shed's shotty teeth.
It's time, let's eat.
When I hoist that stake
its drips got weight
and the sustenance
is changing me.

Light beams split the sky like a mantra
as I and I parted ways. Columns and rows
and those that froze dissipated in a haze

that lingered on into the ages.
While the scribble dilates,
the blind scribe's still turning pages;
coughing up the ink and well
leaving prints like proof,
blew away like smoke
and we're choking
on the documents.

If the mutes
are the mountain,
then the tongues
ain't the foggiest.

Strung up by the atlas
and drooling out like fountains,
I'm carving off the angles
and I'm snuffing all the hatchets.
Breach the frame to take the
balance on from both sides.
Explode. Reside. Capsize
to limber up that flood of limbs.
Get a grip, then sigh.

Blasted by the mud at the bottom.
The bottle, wasted on the shore.
Wet tongue on the gore.

How could I have ever forgotten
the funnel of my battle and the bone in my back.
Dilation of the shell. Degradation of the self.
Sublimation of the water I've been guarding
that I gouged from deep within the well.
I can tell the hounds up in my dome,
they're barking for their hell.
My hand's wrapped around a stone
but I know its home is morose.
Where my robes grow,
the rot clots before the dose
and cinches off at the grief,
with a string of rattling teeth in the trees.

Part bow, part arrow.
Hollow, wanting marrow and oak.
Bones with wires down their core,
swallow the poison and go.
Part bow, part arrow.
Narrows wide and deep.
When it plants itself here.
I can't move. Can't sleep.

Now in my later days I'm a poltergeist, an itch.
A snitch buried in the sound of memories
where the static is a given.

The caliber so intricately
rewritten in the present.

The holes blown wide in the walls
are so much larger than I remember.
So much fodder given to the tinder.
So much farther from the cinders.

So I am the father
of the burr of the blade,
brandished in a blur
by the butcher across
the bloody paper he laid
that was made by the trees,
that fell in the same forest,
that formed the forgotten homes
that future nightmares warrant.
What starved us wasn't underground
and it wasn't the rabbit's warren.
When the bucktooth stardust loosened
we should have taken it as a warning
and flipped the patch up.
Clipped the focus like scalpels to the night light.
Crystalize your blood on bronze plates.

The only sin that exists
is judging the pupil's width.

So listen to the witches kids,
then speak from your own rites
and blow out the candles,
one by one,
and adjust to the dusk,
one tusk,
one tongue.

THE ROOT AND THE ROOF

I was doused in a blanket
of pinholes and fresh scars
as I stood sky clad,
white knuckles quivering.
With daggers raised
the wheel of stars broke,
as their pouring light
caved in the roof.

Into a thick dark pool
I reached my fist
and pulled myself
up by the heels,
now here hangs the proof.

Here's how the ceiling started;
it began at the roots.

From the base near the moss
where sparked the first clues.
Where the first glimmering fang
was the first born to lose.
To be stripped of their fur
and become little more than what
felt like skin stretched for miles.

The clans bid farewell.
But I can still taste the tincture
they placed under my tongue,
as they sloughed the shelter from my body
and pushed me past the tree line.

You are banished but not forsaken.
Disbanded but not forgotten.
Red handed and with reason.
You are brethren of the seasons
that have as yet never come.
This is where you were born
but this is no longer your home.

You were reared by a tribe that no longer
recognizes you as one of their own.
The village is candle light
and bronze as you once were.
But now you are dusty,
you are fire, you are chrome.

You are a horde unto yourself.

This forest can no longer bare the weight
of the volatile temple growing deep inside you.
You are mud crusted, you are shale spires,
you are flow. You are the liquid core of bone.

You are now worth more
than the present elements can afford, so go.

...

And with that I turned,
and stared off into the emptiness
that laid endlessly before me.
I put one foot
in front of the other
and I began to walk.

And as I did, everything
that I had ever known
stretched out farther,
and farther behind me.
Slowly tearing to shreds,
until I was naked,
and cold,
and alone.

A new potential
began to bubble up
from the depths.
A moist fresh breath
began to sigh
from within the wretch…

EMPTINESS IS FORM

Bones will break and disappear,
and skin is never thicker
than the water it contains.

Our organs are simply
lumpy forms of hopes and fears,
and our memories of one another,
are the stains that keep us here.

Our breath supplies the space to seek
the surface down beneath the deep.
Our bones will heat and melt away
and skin will stretch like muted notes
across each other's retrospect,
reaching out towards the strings refrain.

Pain is not the problem,
but our capacity to cope...

So tap the phone and tap the tree
and tap the rope where tension bleeds.

Give way to flow.
Gambit gratitude in towards
the bubbling cellophane of entropy.

What could I be?

A mess of doors and sigils
splintered within the second
prior to their birth.

I have never been here before.
I have never been up to earth.

I am a foreign body
caught within the webbing.
The silken spires monolithic,
white out my sight
the noise reflecting.

Building up upon themselves.
Visions replicating
endlessly within a sphere.
A child enveloped
within terra incognito.

A lot of time and space
and lands so traced,
my life be spent
drawn out by grace.
Still not a drop to taste.

The body chamber still is spinning,
and when it stops the click's a blizzard.
An ineffable hammer we pull back together
until we can hold no more.

Our screams.

      Our laughter.

Our weeping.

      Our songs.

The last sound emitted
from every living being
that has ever been before,
echoes on forever.

And sometimes,
I swear I can hear them all.

BEARS

The sun has gone down
and the night is young.

Street lights blink on.

You can hear the flicker
and buzz in the quiet,
coaxed by the soft winds
running their fingertips
along the hips
of tall buildings.

The shake and spray
of an aerosol can
in a nearby alley.

The sound of small bears
moving in the woods
just out of sight,
beyond the edge
of the trail.

Today,
my heart is heavy.

Sometimes
the only change
we can make,
is in ourselves.

And sometimes
letting go
takes so long,

we forget
that we

are no longer
holding on.

CANYONS

There is a calm volatility,
a discordant harmony,
and an expressive blankness
to all that is.

We do not only write words,
we write the spaces between them.

When we sing and speak
we do not only emit sound
and a message to be carried;

we vocalize and admit a silence,
and a profoundly connecting
inability to be understood.

FIRST, TIE THE LACES

Is it not ok to not be afraid to be afraid?

I am doing my best to be integral, but how can I trust
my tongue when I know it is governed by the entirety
of light and darkness and all that means?

I feel that who I am is created out
of so much which is foreign to me.

Experience and influence, nature, nurture, environment
and that which is within intermingle in such a constant
and intimate fashion, that I have trouble discerning
the facets from one another.

I am constantly faced with myself
in the manner of meeting strangers.

Evolving so quickly like this how can we really ever grow
to know ourselves? How do we ever really know what we
are capable of? Do I just need to trust in that the only
constant in life is that nothing ever is?

I don't want to hurt you,
but how do I know that I won't?

I suppose my greatest struggle right now, is trust.

And I am afraid.

I am afraid that my presence in your life is leaving a mark on you that may never go away, and that your presence in my life is leaving such a mark on me.

Existence is naturally so hazardous.
Nothing can be hidden and nothing is safe.
Every emotion is worn on the sleeve
and every way of being is played off the cuff.
The collar, so beautiful, the buttons so visceral,
the cufflinks, such a ruin.
Such majesty.

And I am so strong, and I am so scared,
and I am so happy, and I am so sad,
and I am so fucking alive
I feel like I am going to burst.

I feel like my being takes up
more space than my body does.

I can honestly admit that I have no idea what is happening to me or why. But I wake up, and I can see and I can touch and I can feel and I may be afraid,

but I can feel myself smile anyway,
and I am ready.

So leave your trace on me,
for my life is not my own.
Please, I beg of you,
mark me and scar me for all
that it is worth and beyond.
Engulf me in your fire.

My surrender is not a choice that I make,
it is a path for which an alternative does not exist.

I am the jungle,
I am the waste,
I am the jewel,
I am the chaff,
I am the sound,
I am the storm,
I am the still,
I am the ground.

I am the spear,
the tincture,
the ether,
the fear and the hope
that foster each other.

OF STONE AND SILK

You will kiss the hand of the leper,
with the same grace and eloquence
that you kiss the hand of the goddess.

For regardless
of the being
within the body
to whom you
bestow this gesture.

You need not
raise your eyes,
to know
that they are she.

ONE LAST TOON

I am poised upon the steeple.
Nothing more than a fragment
of a shadow bent amongst
the waves of people.

My ears, my eyes,
my hands and tongue
grow larger with
every passing day.

Listening closer
and seeing more.

My fingertips maintain dexterity
regardless of their increasing size.
My tongue fills my mouth
until I can't move my jaw.

And I'm starting to feel
a lot like a cartoon.
And the longer I'm alive
the more real it all becomes.

I am not asking to be rotoscoped,
but I am ready for the transformation.

My skull is cracking down the center
and light is whispering out
like smoke within the godly hour.
The silhouettes of us the travelers,
cast wide upon the holy sky.

The trolls and monsters and beings
of a wavering transparency drag their
mammoth knuckles, and cobble stone feet
throughout the landscape towards a single,
converging point.

Where the dark over takes the light,
and the light over takes the dark.
Where we melt into a cacophony
of chaos and calm that slowly
pulls us all apart.

Dimensions are boiled down
into cinders and every border fades.
Our seamlessness, devoid of splinters.
A final glimpse of the primal mists
and the dissipation that remains.

BOOKS ON BENCHES

The raindrops fold

as every page pours
across the sky.

Our silhouettes
strike out across
the horizon,

etching our days
into the fibers of dawn

shadow, by brushing shadow.

Until the night comes,
that sets down our pen
and a new moon
swallows us whole.

TROUBLE MAKERS

Now there's a space

where the gush begins to slow.

The light from the solder is quieting.
The thick vinyl plate of static
upon which we rode is thinning.

Now we're in it to our necks
and speaking like broken cables,
splayed like hands in prayer.

Despite the fray,
the music carries on.

It's funny the times
certain rooms
inside our homes
decide to become vapor.

Everything we touch is sub bass
and blue tones beneath the infrared.
Helmets cast from birch.
Forests of bark no wood within.

Golden rings,
techno gauntlets
in the dark rain doom.
What with which might may,
mix with the craft and cauterize.
Interpreting color like tongues
can sense the speed at which
the distance is approaching.

These hieroglyphs that overlay
everything you see were first found
in the caustic rattling oceans of sound,
washed upon wave forms offered up by
the machine guns that not so long ago
let you know, that I was calling.

PENTAGRAM

Draw your breath forward with
the folding and unfolding of darkness.

Steady your gaze
between the flickering grains
of candlelight and static
basking in tandem
with the wax and wane
of the horizon's iris,
as it gapes and pivots.

Shuddering softly through oblivion
the way the shadow of an owl's wings
pull their cloak over the stretching
form of the rabbit it follows.

Slow your stride.
Relax.

Be consumed,
and find the widening
of narrows within.

ELBOW LAKE

That night I pour you
a hot bath in the clawfoot tub
near the burnt-out truck
in the clearing scattered
with weathered vinyl records.

Balloons drift faintly under
the dim light of the wood fire
and the smoke gripped treetops.

I sponge the dried blood from
your skin, the crusted dirt and
sweat from the corners of your
eyes, and comb the heavy knots
from your hair with my fingers.

I bandage your wounds
and wrap my arms around you
like if I do so tight enough,
there will be no worry
that the next war will ever
take you away.

ZOMBIE

How can
I find more
patience?

BLOSSOM

There are places without body,

unhindered by sight.

Void of the
limits of sense
and the borders
that possible emotion
have come to draw.

Experience has a sharp edge.

Get cut.

Tip,

and blossom like blood that has spilled
in the fountain at the heart of an ocean
                with no floor or surface.

WITH BATED BREATH

An eagle, as it flies
leaves no trace.

An otter
through the water,
barely a ripple.

-

As sand
will fill
the space
created,

so nothing
will consume
the breath
we bated.

TREMULANT

For 2,000 years
the olive tree grows
around my skeleton.

Propped
from
prostrate.

My jawbone
for the weaponizing.

The instruments
between us, played
as if they knew
they were fleeting.

Now it's just
the winds, and
another note in
the wastelands.

WAX

You are the teacher.

I am the student.

Thank you for your patience.

Show me the way.

ROSE

Close your eyes
and feel with your veins.

The skins of countless animals worn
by your ancestors will warm your bones.

The fires they built
have long since been snuffed,
but the visions that emerged from
them are still damp on your skin.

The mythos that drove
the nomads before you,
paint the waking rays
that adorn your rising form
as they blink, in and out of time
with the oscillation of days.

Oral traditions sunk deep within
the mosses and reaching up through
the lamellae of every mushroom
that found a sinking skeleton
and from it,
rose.

You are soaked in the wake
of the ashes and the chanting
of all that have come before you
and they, they become you.

You are the youthful ancient.
You are the resonation of generations.
The adamantium in the crucible.
The feral echo of eternal air.

You are the soft eyes and
calm jaw of mountains of skulls
peering back at themselves.
Remembering what it was
like to be draped in flesh
and strong tongued.
Remembering what it was
like to feel with their veins,

and what it was,
to see a vision
in the flames.

CATACOMBS

Stop trying
to understand
what's being said,
and start listening
to what you're hearing.

WORN

Where have I come from?

The only place and time
I feel I can sincerely ask this
is in those moments
when I am alone
in the dark and silence
because it is here,
and only here,
that I truly listen
for an answer.

And it is here,
that the gods reply.

They are faceless
and respond without words.

They move me like a wick
that has never stopped burning.
But was never lit.

They move me
like a spontaneous gesture
down the limbs of the first sparks,

to find the faint flutter of where
some of the earliest footprints
of my own ideas of myself can be found.

It is a quiet and empty place.
A soft brooding tone
echoing in a dimly lit puddle,
from which a small splash
can now and again be seen.

This is where you've been,
the gods tell me.
This is where you are.

The work you do here
is as important as any
done anywhere else.
It may not be bright.
It may not be lively.
It may not have voice or logic
or reason or language or form.
But there is purpose here.
There is spirit.
There is you.

If we are to walk a road
we must first find where it starts.

But roads of these kinds
and their beginnings,
they are not built.

They are worn.

Not away.

But towards,
and into being.
Until the path
is slowly exposed.

As if it had always been there.

Waiting.

THE FIELD THE WHEAT THE SICKLE THE SWING THE DULLING THE CASH THE INJURY REPEAT

We're not out of touch,
we just know what we're worth.
We keep our shrouds
from the sounds
emitted by the masses
and our fingers on the triggers
of the guns in our purses,
that carry the omens
and curses unseen,
by all but the coins
that catch the light
through the seams.

Flexing their grimace,
as they're knuckled up
and out to the curves
of dark bodies that
creep on like ivory.
Amidst the lustrous poison
and gold-leaf grains; here,
even the cobblestone glimmers.

While on me, fields of pale wheat
sprout timidly from behind my ears

and softly down my back.
Marking the signs of the times
as the flora gets stacked
until the racks snap and crack.

A forgotten mill,
drooling its seasons
out into the dirt.

A gilded dirge
churns in the swamp.

A gluttonous crucible rotting
its bounty upon the branches
of every mourning note played.

The dulling embers of twilight
wail like a mute against the sickle,
sweetly singing as it swings
through the money-grubbing grease.

Cash in hand.
The injury?
Repeat.

The elders bend backwards
and themselves into bridges

as if to mock the saplings.
Babbling in tongues echoing
in tune with the chemical smoke
shredding upwards in ribbons.
Was there reason to their blether?
Was any of this wise?

I once thought I knew,
but now can't be sure.
If our gold was our silence
then the space at the center
of our clenched fists was a blur.

Seizing their lungs, shifting their weight.
Holding their tongues, but wetting their lips.
Turning their sight. Thumbing the grips.
Outlasting the itch and teasing the bait.

But when the henchmen all present
got uneven waistlines that they can't
not keep adjusting then the time for action,
has all but gone.

A single flinch will shatter
the stillness from which
peace had hung on.

COLOR OF THE STAIN

The experiences that you have
when you are completely alone
are holy gifts, meant only for you.

They are songs, hymns of sound
and light and happening
that have waited your entire life
for their moment
in which to spill forward, calling.

APERTURE

The sun
is rising
and you
begin to
feel its
warmth
on your
face,

soaking
into your
clothes.

You take off
your hoodie.

Your hands
are bare.

The concrete
of the skatepark
is still
noticeably
cool.

The crows
overhead
begin
to wilt
the long
shadows,
softly
into
the calm
of morning.

OYEZ

I am hip hop
after it fell
from grace.

>   When it hit
>   the ground
>   not a sound
>   was made.

But the impact was so deep it made
our senses blend together and from
the mixture came a distilled reflection.
In which we found a part of ourselves
that denied all attempts at definition.

-

Now what has died is dead,
and will not be stirred or resurrected.
Reincarnation may raise its head
but its young throat bled,
time again,
will always find a bed
that it has never known.

So take your leave to honor the tombstones.
Then walk away to let the flora over grow.

The predators purring behind you drive you forward.
Curve your teeth around the glass sphere inside
and mourn no more.

The tongue that you've learnt from birth
is out of service. Bathe in the mutiny
of your own capacity to express and
watch the muted soul of presence
as it undresses,
and fades out.

Lights out.
All is gone.

12 o'clock,
and all is well.

INTENTION

Blood may make
the blade holy,

but a tainted blade
can dirty the blood.

FOSTER

When I let go of who I am
I discover who I might be.

Who I will be. Who I am meant to be.
Who I really am. Who I have always been.

I have come to this planet
to engage in a balancing act,
a dance, a battle, with the body,
mind, and spirit of the being
I have been taught to call mine.

This much I know.

I am the ocean, a ship in its waves.
A pendulum swinging heavy,
starboard to port, left to right,
side to side,
slowing.

Once the waves have subsided
the ship will melt beneath the surface.
Once the pendulum finds its center
it will blow away like ash.

Production fosters decay.
Authentic substance is the void.
Emptiness is form.
Formlessness adorns divinity.
Attachment births all suffering.

The usefulness of a vessel lies
not in what it is, but in what it is not.
Let go of everything and see that you
are still here and were none of that.

There is nothing you can take with you
and nothing you can leave behind.
You are beyond. Depth eternal.
None of this, and all of creation.
We are all one.

No separation, no borders, no difference,
no order, no sides, no edges, no ends, no time.

Nothing to prove, nothing to fear,
nothing to gain, nothing to lose.

Mirrors upon mirrors upon mirrors upon mirrors.
Darkness from the light and light from out the dark.

May shattered be thy being, you holiest of scars.

MURDER ISLAND

Your hands fan out
in front of you
like faceted crows,
cawing in the moment
of ignition folding outwards.

Blown into
a thousand
spinning
emeralds
dashed upon
the altar and
deep fountain
of concrescent
collapsing entropy.

Tropical storms
so massive,
civilizations
rise and fall
within the eye,
without ever knowing,
there is a calm
outside the fury too.

SWORDFISH

There are
those of us
who made
a fire,
and used it
to feed
the hungry.

Then there
are those of us
who just
couldn't
get past
how beautiful
the flames were,
and left
the fuel
to burn.

LITTLE BOAT

I have no one to prove wrong
and no praise to bask in.

I have no one to compete against
and that includes myself.

I am the only one on the path I'm on,
and who I used to be
is not comparable to who I am now.

This is a different game entirely,
a new world and a whole other level.

I float with ease, I run my course,
I let my ship to sail to find the winds
as the sea intends.

I am not upon the water; I am of it.

The horizon melts and shifts itself
as fluidly as the sounds that become
the expanse of days as they fold into dusk
inside of night softly beneath the dawn
and on and on through space we turn.

I travel alone in peace with faith
that this is my calling. I am my way.

I know from experience that my strength and light
reflect upon the ocean's surface and act as a signal
to other vessels on travels all their own.
To steer their course, to show no fear.

To find the open waters that cast their names into
the waves where fresh blood and bone and adventure
bid them home unto a cause of constant change.

As the heavens under us come undone,
here we go, row hard my son.

Here we go,
row hard...

Lucky was born in Calgary, Alberta in October of 1985 and has been writing since he was 13.

Poetry has always been a means of release, self-exploration and expression, as well as how he processes and develops an understanding of the world and his place within it.

www.ingramcontent.com/pod-product-compliance
Lightning Source LLC
Chambersburg PA
CBHW062142100526
44589CB00014B/1665